PETER SELG was born in
medicine in Witten-Herdecke,
adolescent psychiatry and psychotherapy. He is the Director
of the Ita Wegman Institute for Anthroposophical Research
in Arlesheim, Switzerland, and Professor of Medical
Anthropology at the University of Art and Society in Alfter,
near Bonn. He is the author of numerous books on the
humanities, anthropology, medicine, education and biographical history. Peter Selg is also involved in extensive
teaching and training activities and the management of public
archives, holding the post of Research Associate at the Col-
lege of Humanities in Dornach.

Rudolf Steiner working on the sculpture of Christ, Dornach 1919

The Figure of Christ

Rudolf Steiner and the spiritual intention behind
the Goetheanum's central work of art

PETER SELG

TEMPLE LODGE

Translated by Matthew Barton

Temple Lodge Publishing
Hillside House, The Square
Forest Row, RH18 5ES

www.templelodge.com

Published by Temple Lodge 2009

Originally published in German under the title *Die Gestalt Christi* by Verlag des Ita Wegman Instituts in 2008

A catalogue record for this book is available from the British Library

ISBN 978 1 906999 01 8

Cover design by Andrew Morgan incorporating photo by M. Schnur
Typeset by DP Photosetting, Neath, West Glamorgan
Printed and bound by Athenaeum Press, Gateshead, Tyne & Wear

'It was my task in Dornach to place within this building of the School of Spiritual Science the central group which depicts the Representative of Humanity between luciferic and ahrimanic powers.'

Rudolf Steiner[1]

Contents

Illustration Credits

Preface

Such wealth I would have—to form an image
that comes close in vision to how he was, the Christ
Friedrich Hölderlin[2]

Over the past three years, through large-scale Goetheanum conferences, events held in various cities and numerous monographs, the Anthroposophical Society's awareness of Rudolf Steiner's Christ sculpture—the 'Representative of Humanity' group—has strengthened and increased. With many people's collaboration, lectures, seminars and publications[3] have examined a wide range of artistic, historical and biographical aspects of this work by Rudolf Steiner and Edith Maryon. Despite this, there is still limited understanding of the significance and origins of the sculptural group surrounding the 'figure of Christ', which Rudolf Steiner called the 'centre' of the first Goetheanum—the School of Spiritual Science which he envisaged. In particular, few have asked what Rudolf Steiner's essential aim was for the sculptural group within the Mystery building he conceived, and to what extent he could regard it as the 'crown' of the building—and, indirectly, as the epitome and emblem of the School. *'It was my task in Dornach to place the central group within this building of the School of Spiritual Science.'*

It is by no means easy to answer this question. As we know, Rudolf Steiner commented on the 'Group' in numerous lectures, explaining its artistic structure and the themes it embodies.[4] Yet he scarcely spoke about the deeper level of his intentions, and about the spiritual requirements of the anthroposophical movement which guided him in this regard.

It was left to each individual to pursue such questions. Since the necessary processes of enquiry are frequently neglected today, and their absence is often, in fact, not even noticed, the 'Christ Group' might easily be seen as a relic of the destroyed first Goetheanum and its sculptural language—in other words as a work of art from a past and now long since out-moded era, as an object of historical value; which is worth preserving professionally and exhibiting as a museum piece—but nothing more. In this view the 'Group' is an element of anthroposophical 'history' or of what people wish to encap-sulate in this history: a world that had its day and is now past.

The situation appears entirely different once one begins to search for *Rudolf Steiner's intentions,* and to hearken once more to the spiritual aims of the Christ sculpture. This path, to which Assya Turgeniev already pointed decades ago,[5] is the one this present study pursues. It leads to Rudolf Steiner and the spiritual focus of the anthroposophical movement. It leads 'into the open' (Friedrich Hölderlin) and into a possible future beyond archives and museums, also for the sculpture itself. Rudolf Steiner conceived a future Mystery site founded on a Christian outlook, at the centre of whose edifice he determined that the figure of Christ should stand, in the midst of the adversary powers confronting it. The Dornach School he founded was to work within this orientation—and in unmistakable terms Rudolf Steiner described the core task of anthroposophical spiritual science as preparing for Christ's reappearance in the etheric. Not only esoteric Christianity but Christ's full reality—his 'form' or 'figure', and his living activity and effect in the past, present and future—were infinitely important for Rudolf Steiner. Although he did not continually speak about this in words, he acted *out of* this Christ spirit (and *for* him, in *his* name and on *his* behalf), doing so also in relation to the School and its real task: that of specifically permeating numerous areas of science, the humanities and life itself with Christ. The central position of the sculptural 'Christ Group' in the 'Johannesbau' (St John's building)—subsequently named the Goetheanum—was in this context not just artistically appropriate but also spiritually necessary. This becomes clear when we penetrate into the deeper aspects of this work. Rudolf Steiner's comment in April 1924 to the architect Ernst Aisenpreis that the sculptural group should be exhibited in the same central position in the second Goetheanum 'as in the first building'[6] is very illuminating in this context. By designing the second Goetheanum, likewise, as a site for future Mysteries with a Christian focus—and (re-)founding the School of Spiritual Science in line with this aim in 1923/24—he was continuing what he had begun ten years previously, in the autumn of 1913. The only question was whether and to what extent the Anthroposophical Society was able and wished to follow him in these intentions. In the autumn of 1920, at the opening of the first Goetheanum, Rudolf Steiner would not countenance placing the Christ sculpture within the building, although it was by then far advanced and this would certainly have been possible. The reason he gave for this was that the time was not yet right, and nor were the members ready for it. He said 'one should wait'.[7] Yet Rudolf Steiner never relinquished his aim of placing the 'Group' in its central position—and how could he? This would have been tantamount to giving up on the founding in Dornach and its goals. The question was merely when the time and the members would be 'ripe' for this to happen—or what kind of processes of preparation would be needed.

Rudolf Steiner died on 30 March 1925, after a long illness, yet unexpectedly and suddenly. It was not just that the Christ sculpture was unfinished in 1925. It was also entirely unclear how the Dornach School that Steiner had just launched and the Goetheanum, intended as Mystery building, could continue without the physical presence of the spiritual researcher and teacher, without the creative centre of the new initiation. The real extent of this abrupt loss, and the completely altered situation in Dornach after Rudolf Steiner's death, is seldom considered. It is overlaid and concealed instead by the conflicts in the Anthroposophical Society after 1925. As early as 1935, now 74 years ago, Count Ludwig Polzer-Hoditz warned that the 'Mystery mood' might very swiftly be lost from the Goetheanum.[8] Marie Steiner, who more than anyone after her knew how to preserve this 'mood' in the sphere of artistic work, was still alive when this warning was uttered. But Polzer's warning prognosis referred to more than the way in which the Mystery plays were staged and performed: it related to the Goetheanum and the School of Spiritual Science as a whole. We can ask whether the widespread sense of helplessness about what should be done with the Christ sculpture and its strange location in the second Goetheanum might not have something to do with the problems addressed by Polzer-Hoditz, and whether the location and the spiritual value assigned to the Christ sculpture might not be a core issue for the Goetheanum's whole present and future, the symbolic yet tangible corner- and touchstone of all developments. Discussions about the possibility of erecting the 'Group' on the second Goetheanum's stage or preserving it in its current sole location, where it cannot emanate an influence through the whole building, are of little relevance in so far as they overlook Rudolf Steiner's real aims for the sculpture and the building, and the possibilities still open (or re-accessible) to the Anthroposophical Society and its School for working towards the christological intentions formulated by Steiner. Exhibiting the sculpture without an understanding of Rudolf

Steiner's intentions for it—and without consensus about how to pursue them further—would certainly not accord with its creator's wishes.

The present volume is concerned with and seeks to briefly engage with these intentions of Rudolf Steiner and the 'figure of Christ' he created for an 'age of extremes'. It arose in the context of an international conference of the Swiss branch of the Anthroposophical Society ('The world significance of the "Representative of Humanity" group. The Christ being in the 21st century'[9]) and takes as its theme contemporary christological aspects of the sculpture. It does so in a very direct manner, and readers should note, therefore, that other contexts and aspects are not highlighted. We know how carefully, modestly and reticently Rudolf Steiner spoke about the 'central figure' of the 'Representative of Humanity' group, and how much he left his audience free to form their own views. His gesture here was one of openness to people of all confessions, in marked contrast to the overbearing, missionary zeal of numerous anthroposophists, which started in the very first years of the sculpture's development and was emphatically rejected by Steiner. This stance of Rudolf Steiner was and remains exemplary for an anthroposophical science of the spirit in which the Christ being is no (illusionary) 'possession' of a specific community with a religious world view, but instead a being active throughout humanity and thus a 'figure of the future'.[10] Rudolf Steiner's repeated words about the 'Representative of Humanity' should be seen in this comprehensive context. But at the same time we should not overlook the fact that for Rudolf Steiner himself the 'Representative of Humanity' was and is the tangible being of Christ—*'Yes, that is the Christ. This is how my spiritual eye perceived him in Palestine, he said.'*[11]

At the beginning of the twentieth century, in fulfilment of

the longing and anticipation articulated by Friedrich Hölderlin,[12] Rudolf Steiner was singularly gifted in developing this detailed perception and giving it sculptural form.

Ita Wegman Institute, Arlesheim
Easter Sunday, 23 March 2008

The first Goetheanum

1.

The Figure of Christ in Spiritual Science

The anniversary of the laying of the foundation stone in Dornach, 20 September 1914

When humanity eventually decides to absorb the spiritual-scientific figure of Christ into the human heart, then the era will have arrived which people long for ...
Rudolf Steiner, 20 September 1914[13]

On 19 September 1914, Rudolf Steiner gave an address on the eve of a significant anniversary: that of the laying of the foundation stone of the 'St John's building', which had taken place on 20 September 1913.[14] Steiner gave his address at 6 p.m., in an atmosphere informed by the war that had started just a few weeks before. In an effort to counter contemporary developments, Steiner had been warning for a long time of the catastrophic approach of this war, which was to seal the end of the old European order. Prepared like few of his contemporaries for this incision in history, and fully aware of its implications, Rudolf Steiner was extraordinarily shaken by the start of the war, and, with a prefiguring sense of the suffering it would lead to, responded to it with deep emotion.[15]

Despite the difficult circumstances at that time, the forthcoming anniversary of the laying of the Goetheanum foundation stone was a significant and celebratory event. The Mystery building conceived in Dornach was to be a vital counter-impetus to the forces governed by materialistic technology (and at the same time nationalist militarism) that were increasingly driving events in Central Europe. The very fact that the building had successfully been started in the last year before the war, and was now well advanced, spoke for itself—even though completion of the great double cupola, which Steiner had long hoped for and emphatically urged, could not be realized by August 1914.

In his evening address on 19 September 1914, Rudolf Steiner wished to prepare the anthroposophists living in Dornach and working on the building's construction, as well as the few members who had arrived specifically to hear the address, for a celebration of this anniversary; he wanted to waken their awareness of the building's historical significance, of the real transformation it embodied. Rudolf Steiner spoke of the events of the war, yet at the same time also of the still existing developmental potential of the human being and the earth:

> A site in the cosmos from which in future sacred, spiritual Christ sunlight will radiate—if humanity wills this, if humanity wishes to make itself ripe for this.[16]

The building in Dornach was to become a Mystery site of the future, a radiating place of human schooling, a sanctuary emanating an impetus for humanity's future. Thus it was to rekindle the purpose of Mystery buildings of pre-Christian times whose spiritual endeavours, rooted in their particular culture, had been of incisive significance for the development of civilization. The 'St John's building' was conceived to serve all humanity, but at the same time every detail of it testified to the Mystery of Golgotha, to the entry of the Christ being into Earth evolution almost 2000 years previously, to his self-sacrificing death and his further work for the future of the human being. Rudolf Steiner's anthroposophical science of the spirit emphasized a Christological core, many details of which he had been describing and elaborating since the beginning of the century. In this sense the building in Dornach—as future Christian Mystery site and place of transformed science, art and religion—was oriented towards a Christological (or Christ-centred) perspective. On 19 September 1914, shortly after the World War had started, Steiner spoke of the 'mission of peace' of Christ Jesus, as a being who 'brings humanity together in harmony', and said in relation to the building:

> We may celebrate the anniversary of a building which most eminently endeavours to bring human souls together in harmony throughout the globe.[17]
>
> If people take the trouble to study the various artistic forms of our building, they will find—alongside all that I have described in lectures here about the purpose of our building's forms—that every detail gives expression to the inclusion and embrace of all human hearts in all nations and races on earth, in accordance with the true impulse of Christ.[18]

On 19 September 1914, Rudolf Steiner recalled the lectures he had given in June 1910 in Christiania (Oslo), about the soul nature of the peoples of Europe and the specific future task of each of them. In previous years he had stressed the importance of recognizing the virtues and connections of these 'folk souls', hoping people would acknowledge them. The Dornach building, too, was entirely 'super-national' in nature, and open for all spiritually questing people from all countries. Its language and elaboration of forms offered a path of spiritual schooling, whose future potential was important for Rudolf Steiner.

> In the forms composing our building we will be able to discern the letters of a language of the gods. And in the

course of humanity's evolution we will learn to speak differently about many things if this building gradually comes to be understood.[19]

Rudolf Steiner's urgency, which had informed life in Dornach since the start of construction, did not relate only to the very limited period before the outbreak of the war, during which it was still possible to build, but also derived from Steiner's conviction that the building devoted to anthroposophical spiritual science must give rise to an effective impetus for peace in a time of tensions and conflicts, as a way towards different developments. As early as 1910, at the end of longer comments on the origins of the world and the human being, and the workings of Christ within these evolutionary processes, Rudolf Steiner had written:

> Humanity began from a unity; but Earth evolution has so far led to sundering and separation. In the idea of Christ we have an ideal that counteracts all such division; for in the human being who bears the name of Christ live also the powers of the high sun being, in whom every human I finds the ground of his being.[20]

In the early spring of 1914, however, war broke out, accompanied by a dramatic level of militarization and emotional browbeating of the peoples of Europe: an aggressive outbreak of—as Steiner put it—'the instinctive nationality principle', which suppressed all spiritual impulses and took a powerful hand in events. In this situation Rudolf Steiner reminded the anthroposophists who had gathered in Dornach of the spirit of the foundation stone laid in 1913 and its historical significance:

> We must be clear that we can only advance by freeing ourselves from this instinctive life. Let spiritual science be a

truth within us. Let us not forget that it is no idle game that we have worked to develop through all the years![21]

On the Dornach hill, at the construction site of the St John's building, anthroposophists from many countries were working at this time: people who were due to be called up to their respective armies at any moment. To them, on the eve of the anniversary of the laying of the foundation stone, Rudolf Steiner spoke about the growing national conflicts and the path towards the future:

> We should learn to distinguish between those who have created the war—not whole nations but individuals, cliques etc.—and those who must tolerate and endure it.
>
> Today I only wish to broach this as a problem of knowledge, my dear friends. Let us build on what spiritual science can give us. There we will find the opportunity, above and beyond all borders, to find our way to each other's soul; and we will grow ever stronger in the forging of this link between souls. We will not grow in strength if we are unjust towards separate nations, if we lack objectivity, but only if, in a real spiritual sense, we find the hill upon which our judgement and feeling stand, just as our building—whose foundation stone we laid a year ago with sacred feelings—stands symbolically upon a hill.[22]

*

The celebration on the following day began with Marie von Sivers's recitation of poems by Christian Morgenstern. Morgenstern had died six months before in Meran. He was one of Rudolf Steiner's most outstanding pupils and colleagues, and had accompanied the Dornach building plans with deep engagement.[23] Suffering from contemporary culture and hoping for developments to counter and redress it,

Christian Morgenstern had noted in his diary as long ago as 1902:

> The longing for a great, shared rite, similar to the great rituals of prehistory, for only such worship can give art its highest aims ... [...] What people call art today is still preparation. As yet the all-embracing hand, the comprehensive spirit is lacking. Increasingly this is permeating our nation, but not yet in an overarching way. We will only have a culture when this nation, incapable of standing still on the path of merely private art, elevates itself to seek a higher expression of its passion for enhancing and heightening life; when it begins, alongside hundreds of thousands of excellent practical and decorative buildings, to dare to create the first building in which it might express its new *soul*. This ideal building will deserve to be called the beginning of our culture. In it the greatest of our painters and sculptors will find their dwelling, and in it the grandeur of poet and musician will establish a home. Until then we are all gypsies [...][24]

When Christian Morgenstern first met Rudolf Steiner at the end of January 1909, and subsequently worked his way ever deeper into anthroposophical spiritual science, he discovered the 'path' he had sought so long and intently. In the summer of 1914 Morgenstern first expressed the wish to visit the site of the developing St John's building, but his death in Meran (31 March 1914) made this impossible. According to Rudolf Steiner, though, it did not prevent his spiritual participation in the fate and fortunes of the anthroposophical movement, which he continued to accompany in his Christ-permeated spiritual soul.[25]

Rudolf Steiner's address on 20 September 1914 took its lead from Christian Morgenstern's poems, as both celebratory prelude and thematic emphasis. Speaking of the turn of the century and the spiritual yearning of wide circles of artists, Rudolf Steiner said:

> If I was concerned, today in particular, to recall Christian Morgenstern, this is to do with the whole way in which, in his own spiritual endeavours and experiences before he joined our stream, he was approaching this spiritual movement of ours. Christian Morgenstern's way of being is in a certain sense just a single instance, a representative example of impulses, of forces and elements, which we can sense throughout contemporary cultural life and which, a year ago today when we laid the foundation stone for our building, hovered before my soul.[26]

Indeed, on 20 September 1913, Rudolf Steiner had spoken of the 'undefined longings and hopes' of contemporary humanity 'for the spirit'[27] and of the longing for an answer born from an authentic science of the spirit. Now, one year later, Rudolf Steiner examined this signature of the times in greater detail. He spoke of the increasing desolation of human souls in forthcoming generations 'if materialism alone should hold sway' and 'if the spiritual impetus of a culture of the spirit does not stream into humanity'.[28] Speaking of the spiritual longing of modern human beings at the beginning of the twentieth century, and emphasizing artists' groups and the latent question of Christ, Steiner said:

> It was painful for me to share the life of these artists who were seeking in the ground of their hearts for something that could re-imbue modern art with spirit. The life of serious artists grew tragic, and this tragic dimension holds true even against the background of world history, since it involved a search for something that can penetrate right

into forms themselves, and because the only true answer to this search is what comes from a real grasp of and insight into the world of spirit.[29]

[...] It is with pain that I look upon the artists who sought content for their art. I am thinking of Carstens, Overbeck, Cornelius: they were seeking to bring the Christ impetus into their art—but in vain. It is worth studying a life as tragic as that of Cornelius, to whom Herman Grimm was so close. He sought the living Christ in the form which Christianity had assumed, seeking something that could permeate his soul and find its way into his art ... Yet he lived at the dead zero moment. Or look at modern architecture: we are still surrounded by the preserved and lifeless herbarium of old styles, with no connection to artistic creativity. Only a living connection with the Christ impulse will be able to give life back to these forms again—but it must be the authentic life of the Christ impulse which imbues forms by virtue of what flowed into human beings through the Mystery of Golgotha. It is not mere talk of this impulse which brings forms back to life; and without these living forms human life is dead, also in the sphere of art.

We have been able to do no more here than make a beginning, both with our spiritual movement and with our building: it is the very first beginnings of a building style that is still to come, that must come. But this is precisely what we are trying to achieve with our spiritual movement: to absorb the impulse of the Mystery of Golgotha into our souls, to absorb it entirely, and to do so in the way in which humanity will need it in future.[30]

Christian Morgenstern succeeded in an exemplary way in absorbing the 'impulse of the Mystery of Golgotha' into his soul during his path of anthroposophical study and school-

ing, as Rudolf Steiner commented in a lecture in Norköpp-
ping a few months before the address referred to:

> In absorbing the anthroposophical teachings he [Christian
> Morgenstern] connected with them in such a soulful way
> that they really became, spiritually, the heart's blood of his
> soul. He absorbed these teachings into his soul in a way
> that for him comprehended and contained the substance of
> Christ. He absorbed them along with the Christ being; and
> the Christ, as he lives in our movement, at the same time
> passed into his soul.[31]

In the course of the celebrations for the foundation stone
anniversary, Rudolf Steiner did not speak further of Christian Morgenstern, and of his great individuality and its future
scope,[32] but instead of the urgent spiritual needs of the time.
In particular he drew attention to Herman Grimm as a person
close to him, and as someone especially representative of
Central European cultural life. Citing among other things
Grimm's historical studies of 'Raphael as universal
potency'—including Grimm's phrase 'We do not know
Christ'—Rudolf Steiner showed contemporary culture's
incapacity to develop a real understanding of history that
would include the Mystery of Golgotha. Reversing Grimm's
phrase he stressed that the question of a true understanding of
the Mystery of Golgotha and of, as he put it, 'the spiritual-
scientific figure of Christ', was central to the construction
project in Dornach. The 'worn-out tones' of traditional views
and accounts of Christ, said Steiner, cannot lead us any further; but 'placing the Christ figure into contemporary culture'
would have great, peace-bringing significance':

> When humanity eventually decides to absorb the spiritual-
> scientific figure of Christ into the human heart, then the era

will have arrived which people long for. They cannot yet perceive the form that Christ must assume if he is to accord with their longings. In pursuing the path that leads to a science of the spirit people will find it possible to speak about the Christ so that life, real content and deep confidence will once more enter human souls—a confidence which is at the same time the certainty of peace itself.

[...] Let us be aware that when we learn to speak about Christ in the right way we also learn to speak truly about the history of humanity. The Christ does not belong to one nation or people but to all human beings. Christ did not say 'You are my brother' to the members of a nation, but to all who belong to humanity. In this knowledge we find our way to every human being and to the peace choirs of all the higher hierarchies—and we find our way to Christ.[33]

This 'stance of soul' as Rudolf Steiner called it at the end of his address on 20 September 1914 was the one he wished to place in the hearts of his audience, or of the members of the Anthroposophical Society, as 'spiritual foundation stone'.

This, my dear friends, must also be a foundation stone which we wish to place within our hearts, upon which we wish to build the invisible building—of which the visible building is the outward symbol.'[34]

Nine years and three months later, at the Christmas Foundation Meeting of the General Anthroposophical Society, and one year after the destruction of the first Goetheanum by fire, Rudolf Steiner would again speak of a spiritual—mantric—foundation stone to be placed 'in the hearts' of anthroposophists.[35] But already in 1914 he used this remarkable formulation in relation to the developing building. The visible St John's building, said Steiner, was founded on 'an invisible building': on a purely spiritual and therefore supersensible form. In the visible forms of the developing building, he said, a spiritual power was at work; and on 20 September 1914 he clearly stressed how this spiritual dynamic was identical with the Christ being:

> May this outward symbol [of the building] at least partly fulfil, though in a still primitive and elementary way, what we sought to beg and invoke a year ago from the universal powers! For our salvation may it come about that people perceive how the spirit that imparted itself to the earth streams through these forms of ours, grasps hold of them, penetrates them with the Christ impulse in such a way that souls are imbued with an awareness expressed in the following words that are still not yet understood in a profound enough way: 'Not I but Christ in me!' May this building—even though it only imperfectly embodies what is wanted—achieve a small degree of what it aims for: to impress on human souls a sense that it is not I, not my own being that falls upon the eye in external forms ... but that the Christ wishes to speak and, through the Word of the higher hierarchies, seeks to come to expression, to manifest and reveal himself ... And this building is to be his 'mouthpiece'!
>
> May the souls who find themselves and each other in the spirit of this building feel themselves permeated a little by a feeling which we can call a connection of the individual human soul with the earth soul ... and by a feeling of how this earth soul lives today, how it has lived since the ancient beginnings of the earth, and how it lives in all human souls!
>
> May this soul feel itself to be the spirit upon the mouth of God: may this soul speak as Christian Morgenstern did:

The animal and plant—these beings possessed
an earthly patience that was not yet human:
what now is just a second was then a year.

But nothing now, for earth, can come too fast.
The human being's impatient growth began,
earth senses: 'Now at last has come the hour

for which I gathered myself through all the aeons!
No longer must I spare my body's power:
for soon as spirit on God's mouth I'll flower'.[36]

In previous months Rudolf Steiner had repeatedly referred to
the developing St John's building as the 'House of the Word'
or the 'House of speech'—as he did also at the opening of the
'Glass House' on 17 June 1914.[37] Now however, in his
address on the anniversary of the laying of the foundation
stone, Steiner was absolutely clear whose 'Word' should
resound in the future building:

> The *Christ* wishes to speak and, through the Word of the
> higher hierarchies, seeks to come to expression, to manifest
> and reveal himself... And this building is to be his
> 'mouthpiece'!

On various occasions, most reticently and as a subtle pointer
only, Rudolf Steiner spoke of the 'spirit of the Goetheanum'.[38] On 20 September 1914, however, it became clear
what the tangible nature of this 'spirit' really was.

Rudolf Steiner began his address on the anniversary of the
laying of the foundation stone with a reference to the poems
of Christian Morgenstern; and he likewise ended it with
Morgenstern's words. This friend, who had died shortly
before Easter, and whose urn stood in his studio, was deeply
connected with Rudolf Steiner's endeavours to create a new,

Christian Mystery site on earth, as messenger and protecting spirit of anthroposophy beyond the threshold:

> Permeated with an awareness of the new proclamation of Christ, he [Christian Morgenstern] bore the new thoughts about Christ evolution and its connection with humanity's evolution up through the gateway of death into worlds of spirit.[39]

The 'Group' in the Hochatelier *(studio), 1916*

2.

'There Will Be Enormous Opposition'

Work on the Christ sculpture and the power of evil

> But what anthroposophy endeavours to bear witness to has very strong enemies inspired by the ahrimanic powers. These powers will grow ever stronger! I want to say this to you today so that you are not surprised when, as the anthroposophical movement seeks to enter the world, it will increasingly have to fight with terrible forces of enmity.
> *Rudolf Steiner*[40]

Soon after the celebration of the foundation stone anniversary for the 'St John's building', Rudolf Steiner, with the support of the English sculptress Edith Maryon, began work on a central sculptural work for the developing building: a 'Christ statue' surrounded by the adversarial powers. In his comments on 19 and 20 September 1914, Steiner referred to this as the 'culmination' of the double-cupola building, of its form language and spiritual dynamic.

From the spring of 1915, in lectures to members of the Anthroposophical Society who were following progress of the work on the building and the sculpture, Rudolf Steiner repeatedly spoke about aspects of the sculptural 'Christ Group' relating both to the nature of the human being and contemporary Christology. After various preparatory studies for parts of the sculpture, as well as the first overall composition, work on the sculpture continued during the war in an atmosphere of destructive forces. Rudolf Steiner gave sculptural expression to these adversarial powers and forces in an audacious artistic and spiritual deed focused on the peace principle of the 'Representative of Humanity'. In his lectures Rudolf Steiner highlighted the artistic challenges and developmental conditions of the work he was creating, but at the same time also the contemporary situation of the battle for the human being and the image of the human being.[41] He referred to Christ's confrontation with the adversarial forces as 'one of the chief tasks of the near future',[42] describing the dangers and challenges of the future epoch of humanity as being of both central importance and apocalyptic in nature. In relation to the forms of the 'Christ Group', Rudolf Steiner repeatedly said that they were derived from immediate spiritual perception.[43] When the Russian artist Assya Turgeniev stood dumbstruck before Ahriman's hands, Rudolf Steiner commented: 'Yes, a great tragedy lies in these hands. I had to modify a great deal in these figures, for otherwise people could not have endured it.'[44]

Rudolf Steiner's whole anthroposophical work bore, at a historically decisive period, both the signature of and the tensions implicit in the unfolding 'Christ impulse'. The 'St John's building' or 'Goetheanum' gave expression and artistic form to this aim and impetus, as the conscious location of a new School founded on spiritual science, whose research and teaching institutions were to develop and disseminate impetuses of Christianized thinking that could seed civilization with new life. Artistic work continued in Dornach throughout the war period, although under provisional circumstances and with ever fewer people. Work never stopped on the 'Christ Group' and the whole building. The scientific research departments, in contrast, were to be re-established after the war, in so far as suitable conditions and new groups of people were found.[45]

*

Rudolf Steiner worked on the 'Christ Group' with Edith Maryon and a few assistants. In February 1917, when he returned to Berlin to give lectures, he told members of the Anthroposophical Society there that he had arrived late because it was necessary 'to advance artistic work on the "Group" to the point where it can now continue without me'.[46] Rudolf Steiner spoke of his (current) absence from Dornach, but to some degree looked beyond this to the uncertainties of the present period of war, also in relation to his personal destiny, and to major tasks for the future. (*'At present it is indeed necessary to think ahead to the future in a certain sense; and it seemed to me to be very necessary, given the circumstances which may develop, to advance this "Group" as far as has now been possible.'*[47]) It was not just since the outbreak of war that Rudolf Steiner knew himself to be at risk: although the efforts in Dornach had been tentative so far, and the work on the Christ sculpture had progressed in a quiet and hidden way, its opposition to prevailing powers and forces was nevertheless clear. The Anthroposophical Society and movement was small in numbers; yet the Michaelic Christ impetus standing behind it (or living and working through Steiner's work) was of innovative and incisive significance—as battleground and sundering of the ways. With the beginning of construction at Dornach and spreading awareness of the developing 'Christ Group', the dynamic of resistance to Rudolf Steiner had increased, and was expressed in polemical articles and texts whose hatred and aggression was growing yearly.[48] In his address on the anniversary of the laying of the foundation stone Rudolf Steiner had quoted words by Vladmimir Soloviev (from 1886): 'I am being literally persecuted, my writings are proscribed [...]. One day

I'm supposed to be a Jesuit, the next a Jew ... so that one has to be prepared for anything at all.' And in relation to himself he added:

> The most varied attacks, from one side or another, have been launched in recent times: I have been condemned as a Jesuit by some, as a Jew by others ... I had to have my baptism certificate photographed because of this.[49]

The tyranny and persecution practised by the Nazi regime did not begin until eight years after Rudolf Steiner's death. But the forces of evil culminating and erupting in German Fascism were already present as tendency during the First World War and in the post-war period, and formed part of the historical reality informing the thinking, feeling and will of people and powers working towards the future in their own way. Already in December 1920 Rudolf Steiner spoke of the tendency developing towards a second, and far more destructive World War:

> People are preparing the next great World War, which will continue to decimate culture.[50]

Although Rudolf Steiner was less concerned about the future of the anthroposophical movement (and himself) than about overall conditions in Central Europe, and from the spring of 1919 worked tirelessly to create new social conditions along threefold lines, he told the members of the Anthroposophical Society on various occasions that the destructive potential of the present and near future would also be directed against anthroposophy and the Dornach building. In January 1921, in Stuttgart, during an internal meeting,[51] he spoke of the determined 'will to destruction' of his opponents. Three months later, in April 1921, he expressed this with the greatest possible clarity:

For a long time now I have repeatedly had to say that the adversarial forces will grow ever more vehement; and this is now certainly the case. One cannot yet say that this opposition has reached its culmination. It has not done so, not by a long way [...]. The powers are still weak which strive to make the forces of renewal, drawn from insight into the world of spirit, into powers of the individual soul. The world has assumed an ahrimanic character [...] Humanity is strongly possessed by powers of evil, by love of evil. And those who today do not understand that we must reckon with this love of evil, and with the ever-growing extent of this love of evil in the battle against anthroposophical spiritual science, will be unable to develop a sense or perception of all the adversarial forces and powers that will arise. For years I have been speaking of this ever-spreading growth of evil. And even if, initially, we do nothing other than form a clear sense of it, this clear sense is also a power and must be preserved. We have to gain clear insight into the world as it is today, as it surrounds us [...]. Efforts are being made to undermine us. It is up to us to work as much as humanly possible, and if the ground is to be pulled from under us and we are to fall through the cleft, our work must nevertheless have been such that it finds its spiritual path through the world. For what we are witnessing now are the last tremors of a world going under; but these last tremors can still be like the wild fury of a madman flailing in all directions. You can lose your life in these convulsions. So we must at least recognize the impulses driving this wild, mad flailing.[52]

Rudolf Steiner wanted to prepare the members of the Anthroposophical Society for forthcoming confrontations.

He was stressing here the character and extent of destructive tendencies, and speaking of processes of destruction whose broader cultural and historical context he had repeatedly described elsewhere. ('*The world has assumed an ahrimanic character [...] Humanity is strongly possessed by powers of evil, by love of evil.*') Steiner was hoping to kindle in his listeners greater awareness of anthroposophy's significance for civilization and its Christological impetus, and with it alert them to the dangerous reality of powers and intentions opposed to this impetus. In numerous lectures during and immediately after the First World War, Rudolf Steiner had spoken about Christianity's evolutionary task within contemporary conditions, about the real presence and activity of the Christ being right into processes at work in society—and at the same time about the enemies of this activity. Without any doubt the Dornach building and its central Christ work of art needed the wakeful alertness of anthroposophists. In London, in the summer of 1922, Rudolf Steiner once more made this clear:

[...] But what anthroposophy endeavours to bear witness to has very strong enemies inspired by the ahrimanic powers. These powers will grow ever stronger! I want to say this to you today so that you are not surprised when, as the anthroposophical movement seeks to enter the world, it will increasingly have to fight with terrible forces of enmity. In a certain sense, our insight into the real aim of anthroposophical endeavours must at the same time lead to us keeping a wakeful eye also on the terrible calumny or other attacks waged by enemies, who do not wish to countenance this movement or let it thrive. But as strong as they may be, the energy of positive human power in each individual must be equal to them.[53]

As Rudolf Steiner pointed out in November 1917,[54] the 'fully conscious battle against the evil arising in human evolution' is part of the task of the future in the sphere both of consciousness and culture. Political developments in the postwar years had further strengthened nationalistic and Communist elements—which, according to Steiner, were respectively luciferic and ahrimanic 'forms of anti-Christianity'[55]—and their real 'hatred of the spirit'. The Goetheanum with its 'Christ Group' was not only located squarely within the tensions of this cultural and historical landscape but also, as 'House of the [Christ] Word', was directly responding to it in preparation for a different kind of future. At the laying of the foundation stone for the building in September 1913, Rudolf Steiner had for the first time spoken the 'reversed Lord's Prayer' from the 'Fifth Gospel', a year before the outbreak of war:

AUM, Amen!
Evil holds sway
Engenders dissolving I-hood,
Trespass of selfhood borne by others,
Experienced in daily bread
In which the will of heaven does not reign
Since the human being sundered himself from your
    kingdom
And forgot your name
You fathers in the heavens.[56]

On the first anniversary of the laying of the foundation stone, Rudolf Steiner once again spoke this mantram in the Dornach joinery workshop. He thus infused it entirely into the being and developmental history of a building which was erected in 'the encounter with evil and its overcoming through spiritual science' (Sergei O. Prokofieff[57]).

After the utter destruction by fire of the Dornach building in the night of New Year 1922/23, the fact that Rudolf Steiner immediately continued work at Dornach and spoke, in addresses and discussions with anthroposophists, almost exclusively of the Anthroposophical Society's failure to protect the building rather than of the work of opponents (or of evil)[58] was completely consistent with his whole procedure and outlook. The presence and efficacy of powers adversarial to Christianity, and also their deeply rooted activity in general trends of civilization, had been clear for many years, and had repeatedly been stressed by Rudolf Steiner. It would have been alien to him to characterize them further or even to complain about them. The anthroposophical community, surrounded by adversarial powers, had failed to protect the Dornach building despite all Rudolf Steiner's warnings. He gave much attention to analysing this failure at the beginning of 1923 in meetings with leading representatives of the Society, appealing for renewed self-reflection. At the same time however he continued the anthroposophical movement's spiritual-scientific work uninterrupted—'*But as strong as they [the enemies] may be, the energy of positive human power in each individual must be equal to them.*'

The 'Christ Group', the 'crowning' of the first Goetheanum, survived the catastrophic fire in a meadow close to the burning Goetheanum. But the building whose purpose it served and in which many innovative courses had already been held by Rudolf Steiner—on general themes of anthroposophy and on the renewal of various spheres of life—was completely destroyed, and Edith Maryon had fallen gravely ill. Despite all these circumstances, Rudolf Steiner continued to work further on the sculpture in 1923 and 1924, whenever he had the time. The symbolic completion of a work of art for a building that no longer existed—as a kind of memorial—

was not Rudolf Steiner's way. Instead, the fact he continued
to work on the sculpture served future ends. The very day
after the fire Rudolf Steiner told readers of the *Basler Zeitung*
that a new building would be erected.[59] Thus the first day of
the new year 1923 introduced preparations for the second
building within the social sphere of the Anthroposophical
Society.[60] At the end of the same year Rudolf Steiner not only
refounded and renewed the General Anthroposophical
Society but sketched the forms of the new building and the
shape of a future School of Spiritual Science. A few weeks
previously (in November 1923) Steiner had responded to the
request of Berlin members by giving them a meditative aid for
meeting the expected apocalypse of the twentieth century.
This was during the time of Adolf Hitler's first attempted
putsch, and it prefigured the forces that were preparing to
send world politics hurtling into 'the dark realms of the abyss'
(Steiner). These verses to the 'Berlin friends', who were to
witness their city consumed by an inferno three decades later,
included the following lines:

> Humanity is forgetting
> The inscape of God,
> But we wish to bring this
> Into the bright light of awareness,
> And then bear over rubble and ashes
> The flame of the gods in the human heart.
> Let lightning strike our sensory houses
> To rubble: we will erect
> Soul houses from knowledge
> Of iron-sure, weaving light.
> And where external things go under,
> There will rise like dawn
> The inmost soul.[61]

Rudolf Steiner continued his work for anthroposophy and the Dornach Christ sculpture to the end of his life—and only a little time remained to him after the Christmas Foundation Meeting. His sickbed stood, finally, directly alongside the Christ figure in his studio. According to Marie Steiner-von Sivers he tried to go on carving it in the very last days of his life. After a severe illness and tormenting encounters with the spirits of darkness and the abyss, Rudolf Steiner died in his Dornach studio on 30 March 1925. The clairsentient poet Rainer Maria Rilke, who also lived in Switzerland and was ill at this time, wrote about this year of 1925:

> Sometimes it seems to me that it is not just this evident face the year turns to me which is so threatening and fateful, but as if this were really the date of a judgment unknown to us but already made, by which the earth has been condemned—I know not to what. I bear the weight of an immense restlessness, and have a sense that if possible we should go on tiptoe, unceasingly, over the remaining ground of this year, so that, whatever happens, its demons don't notice us.[62]

The head of Christ, 1915

3.

Christ Will Stand Beside the Human Being

*Rudolf Steiner and the era of Christ's
etheric reappearance*

We learn that [spiritual science] is something that places huge
responsibility upon us, for it prepares the very tangible event of
Christ's reappearance. Christ will reappear because human beings
will raise themselves to him in the etheric. If we grasp this, then
spiritual science appears to us as human beings' preparation for the
return of Christ. Instead of the misfortune of overlooking this great
event, human beings can become mature enough to grasp the great
moment which we can characterize as the return of Christ. The
human being will become capable [...] of growing into a world in
which the Christ will appear to his newly awoken faculties.
Rudolf Steiner[63]

At the beginning of February 1917, when Rudolf Steiner
started to give lectures in Berlin again after a long absence, he
spoke about the work on the Dornach Christ sculpture and its
context as follows:

And just as [...] Christ walked in physical form at a certain
place on earth amongst human beings at the time of the
Mystery of Golgotha, so it is equally true that the etheric
Christ will walk amongst human beings across the whole
globe in the twentieth century. And if humanity is not to do
injury to the earth's salvation, it must not inattentively
overlook this event. Instead it must be alert so that a suf-
ficient number of people are ready to really perceive the
Christ who will come and who must be perceived.[64]

Rudolf Steiner had been speaking of this preparation for perceiving the 'etheric Christ' or the reappearance of Christ 'in the etheric' (in his etheric body) since 1908, referring to it as the 'greatest secret of our age'.[65] He spoke of anthroposophical spiritual science as a preparation for this event. (*'We learn that [spiritual science] is something that places huge responsibility upon us, for it prepares the very tangible event of Christ's reappearance.'*[66]) Rudolf Steiner had repeatedly pointed to the fact that the forthcoming event of Christ's etheric reappearance was dependent on the spiritual preparation and development of human souls—in other words, that it could not come about without this. (*'The Christ will not come in a spiritual sense if human beings are not ready for this.'*[67]) The adversarial ahrimanic forces were doubtless endeavouring to prevent this return of Christ. In relation to the 1930s Rudolf Steiner said:

> We stand before an important point in world evolution, which we must prepare so that what is to imbue our earth with a new faculty is not trampled insensitively to death.[68]

In certain respects therefore, the work of Rudolf Steiner was comparable with the historical task and mission of John the Baptist, although transposed to a contemporary context.[69] Steiner was preparing for the advent of Christ through his spiritual-scientific teachings, and through the inner preparation of people whose spiritual development he nurtured:

> I want to fire everyone
> with the spirit of the cosmos
> so each becomes flame, unfolds the fiery
> being of his being.[70]

The physical incarnation of Christ and his working on earth had required a circle of people to anticipate the event and to accompany it with some degree of awareness—in other words to place themselves at the service of the newly dawning era. On 30 November 1911, in Heidenheim, Rudolf Steiner spoke about these circumstances and their relation to the task of anthroposophy in the twentieth century:

> Spiritual science, as new revelation from worlds of spirit, brings human beings an understanding of what was proclaimed by the [. . .] call of John, which was recorded in the Scriptures after the Mystery of Golgotha. Through spiritual science [. . .] the human being is given understanding of what Christ Jesus said: 'Lo, I am with you always, even unto the ends of the earth.' Just as a small group of people heard [. . .] the call at that time, in our time likewise there will be few only [. . .] who hear it. But my dear friends, if the call should fall on deaf ears, humanity's evolution could not occur in the way intended by the high spiritual beings. [. . .] Whoever knows how to read the signs of the times will know what it means [. . .] to hear the call of the new, living revelation, or to let it fall on deaf ears.[71]

A little over five years later, in his lecture in Berlin on 6 February 1917, Rudolf Steiner outlined how anthroposophical spiritual science—as spiritual teaching and individual path of schooling—gave people the possibility of entering into a real relationship with the Christ being. In this account Steiner did not describe Christological perceptions and experiences but instead characterized anthroposophy as a faculty of language and questioning. Through anthroposophy, he said, one could question the Christ being—in relation to initiatives and actions undertaken at critical moments in history. Among other things Steiner said here:

Why do we concern ourselves with spiritual science? It is as if we should learn the vocabulary of a language which enables us to approach Christ. And whoever makes efforts to learn to think about the world in the way that spiritual science endeavours, and attempts to exert his mind so that, as spiritual science intends, he gains insight into universal secrets, will find that the figure of Christ comes towards him, emerging from the dark obscurity of the ground of universal secrets. Then Christ will be the strong power in which he lives henceforth, standing by him and guiding him like a brother, so that he can be filled with strength in heart and soul, and be equal to the tasks of humanity's future evolution. Let us therefore not seek spiritual science as a mere teaching, but let us endeavour to learn it as a language, and then let us wait until we find within this language the questions we may ask of Christ. He will answer: yes, indeed, he will answer us![72]

The figure of Christ, according to Rudolf Steiner, emerges as one pursues anthroposophical studies and the path of schooling. He emerges 'from the dark obscurity of the ground of universal secrets' and approaches the questioning person. In other words, he comes towards us in a certain sense. As Rudolf Steiner put it on 6 February 1917, humanity must learn to ask questions of the Christ being, particularly in relation to the founding of innovative ventures ('Should it happen, or should it not happen?'). Christ would then, he said, become audible as 'loving companion', conveying 'comfort' and 'strength', and approaching us to give help and suggestions about what was needed; about what should happen through human beings but in accordance with Christ:

The realm of Christ is not of this world but it must work in this world, and human souls must become the instruments of the kingdom that is not of this world.[73]

According to Rudolf Steiner, the *thought* work of anthroposophical spiritual science, imbued with imaginations, makes it possible to develop a faculty of language and questioning that leads us towards the living Christ. The latter's answer to us will give the impetus for kinds of action that are universally just and cultivate humanity's progress—in the three-level, Christ-devoted path of thinking, speaking and walking,[74] and in the prefiguring of a future which, acting counter to the powers of evil, can further transform the earth into a 'cosmos of love'.[75] Rudolf Steiner was working with this in view, and this too was the focus of initiatives connected with him—as tangible 'instruments' of the coming 'kingdom of heaven':[76]

If you really absorb the spirit of anthroposophy, you will find that anthroposophy will indeed once again open the human ear and the human heart to the secret of Christ. The destiny of anthroposophy aims at the same time to be the destiny of Christianity.[77]

*

On 6 February 1917 in Berlin, Rudolf Steiner said that though the Christ being is not of this world, he aims to work in the earthly realm and needs human souls through whom he can be active in earthly conditions. In 1917 Steiner spoke of human souls as freely acting and thus consciously aware and cognitively focused 'instruments' of Christ. In May 1912, in Cologne, he first described how the Christ being, in the era of his etheric reappearance, no longer needs bodily 'sheaths' but does require organs for his activity. These new sheath organs, said Steiner, are specific and tangible faculties or forces in human souls. (*'All these sheaths are formed from powers that humanity must develop on earth.'*[78]) As path of study and spiritual development, Rudolf Steiner's anthroposophical science of the spirit intended and was able to serve the formation of these 'sheaths', thus preparing the dynamic advent of the 'etheric Christ' by intensifying the necessary powers of soul. In May 1912, specifically, Rudolf Steiner said of this process and the 'sheath'-forces required for it:

> People who can wonder at great insights into and truths of the world of spirit imbue themselves with this sense of wonder; and by imbuing themselves in this way they will in the course of time develop a power that acts as power of attraction for the impulse of Christ. It draws the Christ spirit towards them. The Christ impulse unites with each individual human soul in so far as this soul can wonder at the mysteries of the world. The Christ draws his astral body from all the feelings that have ever lived in Earth evolution as wonder in individual human souls.

> The second thing which human souls must develop and through which they draw the Christ impulse towards them is a feeling of compassion. Whenever a feeling of sympathy or shared joy develops in the soul, this forms a power of attraction for the Christ impulse, and the Christ connects through compassion and love with the human soul. Compassion and love are the powers from which the Christ forms his etheric body through to the end of earthly evolution. [...]

> A third thing that enters the human soul as though from a higher world is the conscience to which we submit when we accord it greater importance than our own, individual moral instincts. The Christ connects with this most intimately: from the impulses of conscience in individual human souls the Christ draws his physical body.

Thus a phrase in the Bible becomes very real indeed if we

know that from human feelings of compassion and love Christ's life body is formed: 'Inasmuch as ye have done it unto one of the least of these my brethren, ye have done it unto me'—for Christ forms his life body to the end of Earth evolution from human compassion and love. Just as Christ forms his astral body from wonder and astonishment, and his physical body from conscience, so he forms his etheric body from feelings of compassion and love.[79]

Christ's etheric body forms from the powers of human love and compassion, according to Rudolf Steiner in the passage above. These powers of love and compassion configure the primary organ of revelation for Christ's reappearance, his *etheric* body:

This is the important advance in humanity's evolution: that before the first half of our century has elapsed, a faculty will establish itself quite naturally in many people that enables them to witness the event of Damascus as personal experience. They will *perceive Christ in his etheric body*. The Christ will not descend into existence in the flesh, but human beings will ascend once they have acquired understanding for the spirit.[80]

*

Immediately after the laying of the foundation stone for the 'St John's building', Rudolf Steiner travelled to Christiania (Oslo) and there, from 2 October 1913, gave his lectures on the 'Fifth Gospel'.[81] These accounts aimed for a 'tangible grasp of the figure of Christ' through detailed and vivid descriptions of his life on earth as Christ Jesus—and also of the path of suffering which Jesus underwent prior to the Jordan baptism, and which made possible the event of the baptism as incarnation of the Christ spirit. Rudolf Steiner repeatedly urged his audience to immerse themselves in Jesus' experiences in a 'living feeling' and in 'deeply sensed concepts', as well as through their (activated) powers of love and compassion:

> What is important is to develop a living feeling of what the soul of Jesus underwent in experiencing what has been described here; to enter with feeling into the pain of loneliness, of endless pain [...]. The importance of Jesus' experience as preparation for the Mystery of Golgotha is something you can come to know not so much through recounting to yourselves or others the events I tried to describe, but really only by gaining a vivid picture which profoundly moves and shakes your soul: a picture of what this man Jesus of Nazareth had to suffer before he could approach the Mystery of Golgotha, so that the Christ impulse could flow into earthly evolution.[82]

Rudolf Steiner's lectures on the 'Fifth Gospel', given immediately following the foundation stone ceremony for the 'St John's building', thus stood doubtless in the context of Christ's etheric reappearance—the development of the Christ's being's 'etheric body' from human powers of love and compassion. It was Rudolf Steiner's intention that his audience in the last year before the war should develop this feeling participation precisely through Jesus of Nazareth's earthly life and, in more circumscribed form, also through the three years of Christ Jesus on earth—in other words through historical recall of the Christ incarnation at the dawn of the new era. Rudolf Steiner turned the inner vision of his audience back to the physical incarnation of Christ with a methodological intent: quite clearly this was to prepare and open the way towards the forthcoming and already, in a certain sense, dawning reappearance of Christ in the etheric:

People will have to exchange the spirit of what is merely thought for the spirit of immediate vision, of immediate feeling for and experience of the spiritually living Christ who walks beside all human souls.[83]

[. . .] From the twentieth century onwards the life of Christ will increasingly be felt in human souls as a direct personal experience.[84]

*

The sculpture of the 'spiritually living Christ walking beside us' and 'approaching' us from a deeper ground was something Rudolf Steiner wished to place centrally in the St John's building, at the eastern end of the small cupola, the real location of the Mysteries. It was intended that anyone entering the building and experiencing its forms and spiritual path[85] would encounter the Christ in the East, the Representative of Humanity, and thus his higher I, his own Christ-endowed being. 'To know oneself as cosmic being, interposed between the powers of the luciferic and the ahrimanic, in *inner, God-sustained equilibrium*',[86] was the requirement and culmination of an inner path to be pursued in the space of the St John's building in an archetypal and at the same time substantive way: 'Not I but Christ in me.'

Thus the human being was to meet the 'representative' or I of humanity. In lectures and personal conversations Rudolf Steiner repeatedly pointed out that each person's individual development in the present and future signified a development towards all humanity, as a new and higher solidarity of human souls—'*because forthcoming human destinies will bring human beings together in a shared mission for humanity to a far greater degree than was previously the case.*'[87] Rudolf Steiner placed the St John's building or the Goetheanum very consciously within the abysses of the twentieth century—as a site of a new humanity based on spiritual schooling. People visiting the Goetheanum and working there were to find moral forces for both their individual and common endeavours on behalf of civilization—forces whose connection with the dynamic Christ being Steiner repeatedly emphasized. (*'The Christ impulse is strength and life, the moral power which imbues human beings.'*[88]) This civilizing work at the dawn of Christ's reappearance was to be configured from the awoken power of conscience of each individual and from new forms of collaboration. Christ, according to Steiner is the future 'Lord of Karma',[89] who sustains and orders human karmic connections and makes possible a mutual relatedness and intensity of common work, which will belong to the social signature of coming times.[90] Through coming to himself in the St John's building or Goetheanum, the individual could also find the other—the You and the higher We. The work and efficacy of the new Mystery site was to be founded on these (developing) forces of humanity, with remembering insight into cultural stages previously accomplished[91] and in an orientation towards the future of civilization—i.e. by accomplishing the path in humanity's evolution that Rudolf Steiner described in detail at the end of 1909 in his book *Occult Science—an Outline*. The book came out in January 1910, in the same month that Steiner began his lectures on Christ's reappearance in the etheric.[92]

*

According to Rudolf Steiner, the Christ figure of the St John's building was 'interposed between the powers of the luciferic and ahrimanic' and brought to expression a human entelechy that had unfolded on earth from the highest cosmic powers. From the very beginning it was Rudolf Steiner's intention to depict in the St John's building the truly incarnated Christ spirit as described in the 'Fifth Gospel'. In one of his early lectures on the sculptural work he said:

> Our particular task will be to form the Christ figure in such a way that we can, on the one hand, see how the being depicted dwells in an earthly human body but how, on the other, this earthly body, in every expression, in all it reveals, is wholly permeated by spirit, by what entered it as the Christ from cosmic, spiritual heights in its thirtieth year.[93]

It was with this in mind that Rudolf Steiner worked on the Christ figure in plastiline clay and (from 1917) in wood. In doing so he was gazing upon the incarnated Christ in Palestine at the dawn of the new era, in his confrontation with the adversarial powers during the temptation shortly after the Jordan baptism. (*'I tried to portray the Christ at the moment of the temptation.'*[94]) But at the same time Rudolf Steiner also spoke of how the completed sculpture would depict Christ 'in his resurrection form'.[95] This twofold orientation or time dimension was something which Rudolf Steiner frequently reiterated when speaking of the Christ sculpture. In various lectures and still more in conversations with visitors, Steiner said unambiguously that he had perceived the portrayed Christ figure in spiritual-scientific vision—as Christ Jesus at the dawn of the new era in Palestine. (*'"Yes, that is the Christ. That is how my spiritual eye perceived him in Palestine," he said.'*[96]) On the other hand Rudolf Steiner not only stressed the resurrection body of Christ that was to be depicted in artistic form (i.e. his figure and form *after* passing through the death Mystery of Golgotha), but also, in his lectures in 1912, already spoke of how the decisive forces of the head of Christ must be formed from the impulses of wonder, compassion and conscience[97]—in other words, from the powers of the *future* soul 'sheaths'. Although much suggests that these three powers were already decisively active in the body of Jesus Christ at the dawn of the new era—and therefore that future formation of the soul sheaths repeats aspects of the earlier (exemplary) bodily formation at a different level—Rudolf Steiner was doubtless emphasizing real aspects of the future in these accounts:

> This portrayal of Christ should really be something like the ideal of the figure of Christ. And the feeling striving towards this ideal, as people will strive for it in the course of evolution, is this: increasingly, in so far as humanity will work artistically to portray the highest ideal through spiritual science, there must be a prevailing sense that you cannot look upon what is if you wish to form the Christ; but instead you must allow to gather strength and work in you, must inwardly penetrate yourself with all that is vouchsafed to you when, through deep contemplation of the spiritual evolution of the world, you experience the three essential impulses of wonder, compassion and conscience.[98]

Thus Rudolf Steiner's remembrance and vision of the past was always also connected with an anticipatory movement. Likewise he gave his (apparently historical) lectures on the 'Fifth Gospel' solely with a view to the future.[99] Christ was and is the 'future form' of humanity.

*

The encounter with the image of Christ in the Mystery space of the St John's building or the Goetheanum was something Rudolf Steiner located very consciously in an 'age of extremes'—in prescience of catastrophes in the twentieth

century[100] and beyond, and in knowledge of the prevalence of
'evil'. When asked where Christ could be found, Rudolf
Steiner replied: 'Where affliction is greatest'. The twentieth
century was to highlight the reality of this phrase in the most
diverse ways—people were vouchsafed Christ experiences at
times of the greatest affliction and horror, encountering the
Christ in apocalyptic circumstances such as Stalingrad:

> [. . .] The Christ will stand beside the human being as his
> counsellor. This is not meant as image alone: people will
> really receive the advice they need from the living Christ,
> who will be both counsellor and friend to them, speaking to
> human souls like a person walking beside us.[101]

Rudolf Steiner conceived the building at Dornach as the
site of future Mysteries, as place of initiation or building of
sacramental knowledge. Here human beings were to pursue
authentic spiritual paths and prepare themselves for their
civilization-nurturing work—and thus also for the encounter
with evil and for its real overcoming. The garment of the
Christ figure in the small cupola was to be formed of
'streaming love' alone;[102] and Rudolf Steiner often said that
the Christ being did not combat the adversarial powers or
judge them, but really overcame them with his power of
love.[103] The human being was not only intended to come
close to this Christ figure in the St John's building or
Goetheanum, but also to merge with it—in a conscious,
cognitive sense, as Rudolf Steiner accentuated after the
destruction of the wooden, double-cupola building:

> At Ephesus the statue of the gods; here at the Goetheanum
> the statue of the human being, the statue of the Repre-
> sentative of Humanity, of Christ Jesus. Identifying with
> him it would be our aim, in all modesty, to be subsumed in

knowledge as once, in their own way, which is no longer wholly comprehensible to humanity today, the pupils at Ephesus merged with Diana of Ephesus.[104]

According to Rudolf Steiner, the Goetheanum was to be the site of the new, curative Mysteries—the Christian Mysteries of a dawning future.

He steadfastly preserved this future focus even after the catastrophe of the fire and the wholesale destruction of the building. He performed the Christmas Foundation Meeting, founded the esoteric School of Spiritual Science (with its various faculties dedicated to different realms of life), designed the forms for a second building to be created in concrete—and continued working on the Christ sculpture. In October 1923, ten months *after* the destruction of the first Goetheanum, Rudolf Steiner spoke for the first time of Mystery plays which (at some future point) were to be performed at Easter in front of the Christ sculpture ('. . . *if in the future it should also prove possible to set a living drama before this sculptural element, precisely at Easter—a living, dramatic performance*'). At the same time he said, among other things:

A kind of Mystery play should unfold specifically within this sculpture and these architectural forms. Its chief personae would be the human being and Raphael, Raphael with the staff of Mercury, and with all that relates to and is associated with it. In the realm of living art everything, everything makes legitimate demands; and basically there is no sculpture and no architecture which, if its core is cosmic truth, would not exert demands on what occurs artistically in a space that has such architecture and sculpture. And at Easter this architecture and this sculpture would demand a mystery play: this would depict the human being, taught by Raphael to recognize the degree to which the ahrimanic and luciferic powers make him ill and the degree to which the power of Raphael can instruct us in understanding and perceiving the healing principle, the great, universal therapy which lives in the Christ principle.[105]

With this orientation and despite the 'prevalence of evil', Rudolf Steiner continued to face forward to the end, serving the Christian mysteries and their moral will—for a perpetuation and renewal of Creation.[106]

> So that good may grow
> from everything that we
> start from our hearts,
> from everything that we
> try through our heads
> to guide purposefully...[107]

Rudolf Steiner never wavered from this aim *'for on all this the Goetheanum was predicated and established...'*[108]

*

Rudolf Steiner doubtless hoped that this developmental momentum would continue after his death. The Goetheanum was a house of the Christ Word. In his farewell words to his disciples Christ had said: 'And whatsoever ye shall ask in my name, that will I do, that the Father may be glorified in the Son. If ye shall ask any thing in my name, I will do it.' (John 14: 13–14). Rudolf Steiner served the Christ spirit and promised those connected with him his continuing support after his death—those too with whose help (or through whom) *he* intended to direct the esoteric sections of the School of Spiritual Science in Dornach.[109] World-changing impulses were intended to proceed from the sections of the School in

Dornach—initiatives for christianizing science as well as social, artistic and religious life. These impulses were to proceed from the house of the Christ Word and the Christ sculpture:

> It was my task in Dornach to place within this building of the School of Spiritual Science the central group which depicts the Representative of Humanity between luciferic and ahrimanic powers...[110]

Just as on cloudy days we may forget
the sun—and yet unceasingly it still
shines luminous: so in gloomy times
we may sometimes forget you; but
ever and again we're stunned, and even
blinded by your inexhaustible, your bright
sun spirit that keeps forever shining
upon us wanderers in the dark.[111]

Christian Morgenstern: 'For Dr Rudolf Steiner'

Appendix: Work on the Group

A manuscript written in 1928[112]
by Assya Turgeniev

When Edith Maryon arrived in Dornach in February 1914, the outlines of the first Goetheanum were indicated only by a framework of two intersecting, circular scaffolds. At the time the group of members involved in the building was very small still—the architects, a few artists—yet the sound of hammers echoed from the hill far into the surrounding region, and hundreds of workers were planing timbers in the joinery workshop. Behind this, in a small studio that was already almost filled to bursting with models of the Goetheanum, Miss Maryon began to enlarge Rudolf Steiner's designs and to prepare moulds made of Dornach clay for the concrete casting. Always calm and happy she soon found her way easily into the initially very primitive conditions. The only thing that marked her out was a certain distance which she kept from her colleagues—as if she felt herself to be carried by awareness of the great task she must fulfil.

Soon after her arrival, with a quiet, reverent pride, Miss Maryon showed us the first sculptural designs by Rudolf Steiner for the wooden Group which was to form the central focus of the Goetheanum. From the immediacy of expression of these models quickly made in plastiline all of us could sense that here too a great work was underway. Everyone at the Goetheanum wished to place his skills at the service of Rudolf Steiner's undertakings, but perhaps Edith Maryon knew best how to devote her artistic ambition, if one may call it that, wholly and unreservedly to being nothing more than the pupil and serving hand of Rudolf Steiner. This was more difficult and a rarer thing than the lapse of time may now make it seem. Not only did she understand that the classical training she had wholly mastered, and also her artistic achievements, could not be adequate where entirely new impulses were to enter humanity, but she was also able to act accordingly, without hesitation, and it is in this that Edith Maryon's immeasurable service lies. Dr Steiner never needed to fear any unexpressed feelings of hurt on her part when, with a strong grasp, he reshaped her so delicately modelled studies: she left him entirely free, and only reluctantly and obediently added her name to the small model, alongside his.

It was in the spring of 1916 that Miss Maryon first showed us the head of the Representative of Humanity modelled by Dr Steiner in plastiline. 'This is how he was,' she said, repeating to us Dr Steiner's own words, 'but the turn of the head is not right: one should not see too much of the neck, for there is no pride in him.'

Sometimes she would call one or other of us to her—by now she was in the large Group studio—to study a muscle or arm movement. But in the execution, of course, all outward resemblance vanished. For us, however, it was a very good opportunity to glimpse the development of the 'Group' in the strictly protected studio. Between the beams of the scaffold one could discern a few forms reminiscent of the Goetheanum architraves; but here, as though in the grip of a storm, they clenched and clustered together to create living being. After a good hour spent lying on the stairs, head downwards in imitation of the falling Lucifer, one was allowed to view his progress. These preparatory studies by Miss Maryon were certainly classically beautiful and also strong in impact; but after a couple of weeks, when the opportunity arose, it was a shock to see the model once more: as if an elemental force now spoke from the tragic mask of the falling figure, and the classical features of the other were enveloped in a sultry updraught sucking him away from gravity. The eye could no longer merely rest on the lovely form itself but now, after Rudolf Steiner had taken a hand in its further elaboration, lived with it, passed through it, as the form itself vanished to become, one may say, pure movement, expression, being. 'I could not make them entirely as they are,' he said. 'This distortion of the human as it is in reality cannot be shown to people, for they could not endure it.'

On one occasion Miss Maryon tried to tense her muscles somewhat to show us the movement of the Christ. 'It is not so,' said Dr Steiner, stopping her. 'There must be nothing combative. You must keep your hands very loose, and calm.'

Then the moment arrived when the model was finished. Around Christmas 1917, free of scaffold, it was shown to Dornach residents. Dr Steiner stood next to it on the stairs. He seemed inwardly moved, attentive to how people would respond to the work, and his words sounded like answers to our unexpressed questions. My gaze was held by the simultaneously grasping and pulling arm movement of Ahriman. 'Yes, a great pain, a great longing lies in this movement,' said Dr Steiner. (Certainly one can only recall an approximation of some of the things Dr Steiner said about the Group on this and other occasions.) 'Everything is clenched and cramped in Ahriman: he wants to make everything crooked, hard, cartilaginous and bony. If you feel your way into these qualities you will get a sense of his organism. This is also why he is smaller than an ordinary person, just as Lucifer is larger. Imagine an organism consisting only of blood-warmth, air and lungs—then you have Lucifer. He wishes to evaporate, to spread and be diffused: the blood rises into his head, inverts in the lobes of the lungs, which are also ears. He hearkens to cosmic music, catching the sound ether with these lobes. And at the very centre, where all the forms of the one and the other meet, you find the figure of the Representative of Humanity. Also in the whole way that the surfaces are worked. It is a matter for each individual's personal freedom to take this figure as Christ: he does not impose himself. He does not judge but is simply there. Nothing aggressive should be felt in his gesture, which also comes to expression in everything: the forms of the body, the asymmetry of the features, and in the surface forms. The new element here is to pass from form to movement. He walks calmly forwards; the others cannot endure his proximity, and thus judge themselves. Not by the hand of Christ, but by proximity to him, Lucifer breaks his own wings and Ahriman chains himself in the gold veins of the earth. At the side you have each as they are in their own intrinsic nature, untouched by the power of Christ. There is much tragedy in this relationship of the two to each other. And up there—only added later—is the onlooker, a being who has nothing to do with the earth. He has come from the cosmos and gazes into earthly events. And here you see how the features of the face are affected by the stance.'

The intensity of this model's effect could be compared to the power of a natural phenomenon. One only found calm again in the central figure walking upon the waves. At such moments one could come to a truer apprehension of our times. Humanity's search through the centuries, from primitive Romanesque reliefs of the Last Judgment through to Michelangelo's work, here found its answer.

I was told that Frau Doctor Steiner had asked to hear a legend about the Group; and one evening, in the joinery workshop, Rudolf Steiner related the new Isis legend.

Through the long years of the war our wood-carving group grew ever smaller. Far distant from each other, just four hammers kept the work going in the cold, dark rooms of the scaffolding-filled Goetheanum. And it was our destiny to be asked to help on the Group. For a while a fifth person worked amongst us, perhaps worked best of all, but only for a short time.

Enormous blocks of wood stood before us, piled in layers on each other, and now it was our job to make measurements, and tremble as we did so. 'No more than two centimetres' was the command that hung over us like a sword of Damocles: the depth to which we were permitted to take the preparatory work. And to the point of despair, likewise, we walked about with a long, flexible metering needle, fixed to a board, from the workplace to the model, to find a particular point; while behind us Miss Maryon also trembled, rightly, in concern for her two centimetres. She herself was working on the central figure. Glorious like a figure of Apollo, with beautifully rounded muscles carved soft as satin in the wood, the sculpture stood there when Dr Steiner arrived back after a long trip. 'But this English Lord is not my Christ,' he laughed. 'My Christ is not so muscular: he is not plump.' And energetically his chisel drove into the lovely work. Miss Maryon showed not the slightest trace of dissent or injured feeling.

Dr Steiner was cheerful and relaxed as he worked, and also liked to talk at the same time, or to tell a joke. Now and then he came to one or another of us to encourage or give advice. 'He's a fine man,' he comforted me as I was working on the so-called small figure of Ahriman. 'It is a fine thing if the ugly is made ugly. Then it is true. People will have to take more and more account of ugliness in art ... You need to keep flexible with your left hand the whole time, feeling into the form with the chisel: always looking for the movement of the surface not its boundary. Feeling inhabits the left hand, while you give strength with the right. Here too you can round things, it is not like the architraves: Lucifer should be carved polyhedrally ...'

'Ahriman is a powerful Lord,' he said on another occasion. 'I have only been able to hint at these things: he influences and works on the surroundings, imbuing them with himself. Behind him in the cave one must engrave his negative profile as shadow, and in the rocks, scattered around, one should pick out hints of his emerging facial features. Everywhere nature strives to form a face. That is its aim. When I'm walking outside I continually see faces trying to emerge.'

It was always a moment of great celebration for us when a piece that had been fully prepared was sent over to Dr Steiner in the other studio. There, in great seclusion, he worked on the central figure, and undertook the final execution of our preparatory work. But unfortunately this happened far too little. Everywhere one can see places in the Group where his hand, working from inner vision and experience, enhanced the power of expression and character of the forms. Our powers were very inadequate, and this was something per-haps that Miss Maryon felt most intently, finding herself too bound by an over-rigid academic training. Thus the work slowly proceeded, with trouble and joy. We inscribed the wood with our deficiencies and achievements until, in places, the ever-threatening two-centimetre boundary was reached— or sometimes, with Dr Steiner's help, exceeded. In the meantime, the sculptural work in the Goetheanum had been completed by artists returning from the war, and the building was in a state that allowed courses and performances to take place there. The Group was also waiting to be put together in its location, so that various parts could be worked on with a view to their effect from a distance, and any disturbing anomalies integrated into the whole. Yet Miss Maryon expressed reluctance about our wish to see the Group in the surroundings created for it. There was still time, she said, there was no hurry . . . It was true that the building could not be fully completed without the Group, nor inaugurated. But we already knew from Dr Steiner that neither we nor the time were ripe for the building to be inaugurated. It leaves us with a question that the Group—unfinished as it is as single piece, yet encompassing and embodying the whole building—was preserved for us from the New Year's fire.

On one occasion I had something to attend to in Dr Steiner's studio. He was there and was looking at the work just done on the central figure. The whole body was already emerging from the sheath of the preparatory stage, ensouled, breathing and warm. 'Flowers are our greatest teachers in sculpture, and this is why one should not model them,' Dr Steiner said often, and the whole surface treatment also struck me as flower-like. In the rarest, greatest works of humanity we find this complete dissolving and resolution, this transparency of matter achieved through artistic form. Yet here form had assumed soul. 'I sought to bring soul into it everywhere,' said Dr Steiner. 'The ancients, drawing on impulses of wisdom, sculpted in stone. Christian sculpture must engrave warmth into the living material of the wood. In this way the dead can also see it.' For a long time we stood there, and as though sensing a question from him I dared at last to say: 'It is beautiful Herr Doktor.' So deep was the humility of one who had achieved such great things, that he took pleasure at my remark.

Notes

All quotations from Rudolf Steiner have been translated from the original German sources. A list of referenced works that have been published in English as complete 'GA' (*Gesamtausgabe* or Collected Works) titles are given on p. 70.

1. Rudolf Steiner, GA 192, lecture of 9 June 1919.
2. Friedrich Hölderlin, 'Patmos', in: *Sämtliche Werke und Briefe* [Collected works and letters] ed. Michael Knaupp, vol. I, Munich 1992, p. 171.
3. Recent publications on this theme include: Peter Selg, *Edith Maryon, Rudolf Steiner und die Dornacher Christus-Plastik*, Dornach 2006; Andrea Hitsch, 'Historische Augenblicke. Die beiden Goetheanum-Bauten und die Frage nach dem Standort der "Gruppe des Menschheitsrepräsentanten"', in *Stil*, issue 2, 2007; Judith von Halle, *'Das Christliche aus dem Holz herausschlagen'. Rudolf Steiner, Edith Maryon und die Christus-Plastik*, Dornach 2007; Judith von Halle and John Wilkes, *Die Holzplastik des Goetheanum. 'Der Menschheitsrepräsentant zwischen Luzifer und Ahriman'*, Dornach 2008. Mirela Faldey has compiled an extensive documented monograph on the history of the Group's development, and this is due to be published shortly with the support of the Swiss branch of the General Anthroposophical Society.
4. See Peter Selg, *Edith Maryon, Rudolf Steiner und die Dornacher Christus-Plastik*, Dornach 2006, pp. 72–114.
5. See Assya Turgeniev, *Was wird mit dem Goetheanum-Bau geschehen?*, Basel 1956.
6. Quoted in Andrea Hitsch: 'Historische Augenblicke. Die beiden Goetheanum-Bauten und die Frage nach dem Standort der "Gruppe des Menscheitsrepräsentanten"', in *Stil*, issue 2, 2007, p. 49.

7. Quoted in Assya Turgeniev, *Was ist mit dem Goetheanum-Bau geschehen?*, Basel 1956, p. 26.
8. Count Ludwig Polzer-Hoditz, Goetheanum talk on 14 April 1925, in Emanuel Zeylmans van Emmichoven, *Wer war Ita Wegman. Eine Dokumentation, vol. 3*, Dornach 2000, p. 336. (Translated as: *Who Was Ita Wegman*, vol. 3, Mercury Press, 2006).
9. Goetheanum, Dornach, 31 January to 3 February 2008.
10. Rudolf Steiner, GA 13, chapter 'Man and the Evolution of the World'.
11. Quoted by Willem Zeylmans van Emmichoven in: Peter Selg, *Anfänge anthroposophischer Heilkunst*, Dornach 2000, p. 191.
12. See in particular Hölderlin's hymns 'Patmos', 'Friedensfeier' ['Celebration of peace'] and 'Der Einzige' ['The sole one'], as well as studies relating to these by Eduard Lachmann, *Hölderlins Christus-Hymnen*, Vienna 1951; Ulrich Hässermann, *Friedensfeier. Eine Einführung in Hölderlins Christus-Hymnen*, Munich 1959; and Heinrich Buhr, *Hölderlin und Jesus von Nazareth*, Pfüllingen 1977.
13. Marie Steiner (ed.), *Die Sehnsucht der Seelen nach Geist. Ein Zeichen der Zeit. Worte Rudolf Steiners am ersten Jahrestag der Grundsteinlegung des Goetheanum in Dornach am 20. September 1914*, Dornach 1938, p. 17.
14. See Rudolf Steiner's address for the laying of the foundation stone in Rudolf Steiner: GA 268.
15. See the relevant testimonials in Peter Selg, *Die Kultur der Selbstlosigkeit. Rudolf Steiner, das Fünfte Evangelium und das Zeitalter der Extreme*, Dornach 2007, pp. 14 f.
16. Marie Steiner (ed.), Rudolf Steiner: *Schicksalszeichen auf dem Entwickelungswege der Anthroposophischen Gesellschaft*, p. 36.
17. Ibid., p. 37.
18. Ibid.
19. Ibid.
20. Rudolf Steiner, GA 13.
21. See Marie Steiner (ed.), Rudolf Steiner, *Schicksalszeichen auf*

dem Entwickelungswege der Anthroposophischen Gesellschaft, p. 36.

22. Ibid., p. 45.

23. See Peter Selg, *Christian Morgenstern. Sein Weg mit Rudolf Steiner*, Stuttgart 2008.

24. Quoted in Michael Bauer, *Christian Morgensterns Leben und Werk*, completed by Margareta Morgenstern and Rudolf Meyer, with contributions from Friedrich Kayssler, Munich 1933, pp. 160 f.

25. See Peter Selg, *Christian Morgenstern. Sein Weg mit Rudolf Steiner*, Stuttgart 2008.

26. Marie Steiner (ed.), *Die Sehnsucht der Seelen nach Geist. Ein Zeichen der Zeit. Worte Rudolf Steiners am ersten Jahrestag der Grundsteinlegung des Goetheanum in Dornach am 20. September 1914*, p. 5.

27. Rudolf Steiner, GA 268, chapter 'Ansprache zur Grundsteinlegung des Dornacher Baues 20 September 1913'.

28. Marie Steiner (ed.), *Die Sehnsucht der Seelen nach Geist. Ein Zeichen der Zeit. Worte Rudolf Steiners am ersten Jahrestag der Grundsteinlegung des Goetheanum in Dornach am 20. September 1914*, p. 7.

29. Ibid., p. 12.

30. Ibid., p. 30.

31. Rudolf Steiner, GA 155, lecture of 14 July 1914.

32. See Peter Selg, *Christian Morgenstern. Sein Weg mit Rudolf Steiner*, Stuttgart 2008.

33. Marie Steiner (ed.), *Die Sehnsucht der Seelen nach Geist. Ein Zeichen der Zeit. Worte Rudolf Steiners am ersten Jahrestag der Grundsteinlegung des Goetheanum in Dornach am 20. September 1914*, p. 17.

34. Ibid., p. 20.

35. See Rudolf Steiner, GA 260. For the spiritual-organic background to this foundation stone laid 'in the heart' see also Peter Selg, *Mysterium cordis. Von der Mysterienstätte des Menschenherzens. Studien zu einer sakramentalen Physiologie des*

Herzorgans. Aristoteles, Thomas von Aquin, Rudolf Steiner, Dornach 2006. In relation to the events of the laying of the foundation stone at the Christmas Foundation Meeting 1923/ 24, see Sergei O. Prokofieff, *May Human Beings Hear It!,* Temple Lodge Publishing, 2004.

36. Marie Steiner (ed.), *Die Sehnsucht der Seelen nach Geist. Ein Zeichen der Zeit. Worte Rudolf Steiners am ersten Jahrestag der Grundsteinlegung des Goetheanum in Dornach am 20. September 1914,* pp. 20 f.

37. See Rudolf Steiner, GA 286, lecture of 17 June 1914.

38. In this regard see Rudolf Steiner's reply to the speech of thanks by Louis Werbeck at the end of the Christmas Foundation Meeting, where he said, among other things: 'But my dear friends, I knew I might say what has occurred here, for it was said in full responsibility and cognizance of the spirit that is and should be present as the spirit of the Goetheanum. In its name I have allowed myself to say certain things during these days that could not have been expressed so strongly if not spoken with an eye cast upwards to the spirit of the Goetheanum, to the good spirit of the Goetheanum. And so let me also accept these words of thanks on behalf of the spirit of the Goetheanum, for which we wish to work, strive and act in the world.' (Rudolf Steiner, GA 260, chapter 'Dankesworte aus dem Mitgliederkreis und abschliessende Worte Rudolf Steiners').

39. Marie Steiner (ed.), Rudolf Steiner, *Christian Morgenstern. Der Sieg des Lebens über den Tod,* Dornach 1935, p. 100.

40. Rudolf Steiner, GA 211, lecture of 24 April 1922.

41. Peter Selg, *Edith Maryon, Rudolf Steiner und die Dornacher Christus-Plastik,* Dornach 2006, pp. 73 ff.

42. Rudolf Steiner, GA 165, lecture of 28 December 1915.

43. 'It is not a question of making a merely emblematic representation but rather that every single trait in the three beings is created in the very minutest detail from spiritual-scientific vision.' (Rudolf Steiner, GA 157, lecture of 10 June 1915.)

44. Assya Turgeniev, 'Aus der Arbeit an der Gruppe' (1928). See pp. 53–59 of this book.

45. See Friedrich Rittelmeyer, *Meine Lebensbegegnung mit Rudolf Steiner*, Stuttgart 1983, p. 128. (Translated as: *Rudolf Steiner Enters My Life*, Floris Books 1982.)

46. Rudolf Steiner, GA 175, lecture of 6 February 1917.

47. Ibid.

48. See Rudolf Steiner, GA 255b.

49. Marie Steiner (ed.), *Die Sehnsucht der Seelen nach Geist. Ein Zeichen der Zeit. Worte Rudolf Steiners am ersten Jahrestag der Grundsteinlegung des Goetheanum in Dornach am 20. September 1914*, p. 18.

50. Rudolf Steiner, GA 202, lecture of 25 December 1920.

51. Notes by Karl Stockmeyer, quoted by Alexander Lüscher, in Rudolf Steiner, GA 255b, Introduction.

52. Rudolf Steiner, GA 204, lecture of 17 April 1921.

53. Rudolf Steiner, GA 211, lecture of 24 April 1922.

54. Rudolf Steiner, GA 178, lecture of 18 November 1917.

55. Rudolf Steiner, GA 198, lecture of 3 April 1920.

56. Rudolf Steiner, GA 268, lecture of 20 September 1913. The German original is:

> *Aum, Amen!*
> *Es walten die Übel*
> *Zeugen sich lösender Ichheit*
> *Von andern erschuldete Selbstheitschuld,*
> *Erlebet im täglichen Brote,*
> *In dem nicht waltet der Himmel Wille,*
> *Da der Mensch sich schied von Eurem Reich*
> *Und vergass Euren Namen*
> *Ihr Väter in den Himmeln.*

57. Sergei O. Prokofieff, *The Encounter with Evil and its Overcoming through Spiritual Science*, Temple Lodge Publishing, 1999.

58. See Rudolf Steiner, GA 259.

59. Replying to the newspaper reporter's question 'Will you

consider rebuilding?' Rudolf Steiner said: 'Definitely!' Then
he explained the nature of insurance cover for the building,
and said that the insurance sum payable would only cover a
part of actual expenditure. He concluded with the words: 'I
will therefore have to build in a different and more modest
way, and no longer in wood. But the basic artistic orientation
will be retained.' (In: Rudolf Steiner, GA 259, interview of 1
January 1923.)

60. See Rudolf Steiner, GA 259; and also Peter Selg, 'Rudolf
Steiner und das zweite Goetheanum', in Peter Selg, *Vom
Umgang mit Rudolf Steiner's Werk. Ursprung, Krise und
Zukunft des Dornacher Goetheanums*, Dornach 2007, pp. 21 ff.

61. Rudolf Steiner, GA 268, meeting on 8 February 1923.

62. Letter to Marie von Thurn und Taxis, 17 September 1925.
Quoted in: Peter Selg, *Rainer Maria Rilke und Franz Kafka.
Lebensweg und Krankheitsschicksal im 20. Jahrhundert*, Dor-
nach 2007, p. 83.

63. Rudolf Steiner, GA 118, lecture of 25 January 1910.

64. Rudolf Steiner, GA 175, lecture of 6 February 1917.

65. Ibid.

66. Rudolf Steiner, GA 118, lecture of 25 January 1910.

67. Rudolf Steiner, GA 200, lecture of 31 October 1920.

68. Rudolf Steiner, GA 118, lecture of 13 March 1910.

69. Peter Selg, *Das Ereignis der Jordan-Taufe. Epiphanias im
Urchristentum und in der Anthroposophie Rudolf Steiners*,
Stuttgart 2008.

70. Rudolf Steiner, GA 40.

71. Rudolf Steiner, GA 127, lecture of 30 November 1911.

72. Rudolf Steiner, GA 175, lecture of 6 February 1917.

73. Ibid.

74. See Rudolf Steiner's text on the spiritual guidance of
humanity (1911; GA 15) as well as his fundamental lecture on
7 March 1914 in Pforzheim (in Rudolf Steiner, GA 152).

75. See Rudolf Steiner, GA 13.

76. See in this connection my illustrative monograph: Peter Selg,

Die Arbeit des Einzelnen und der Geist der Gemeinschaft.
Rudolf Steiner und das 'soziale Hauptgesetz', Dornach 2007.

77. Rudolf Steiner, GA 226, lecture of 17 May 1923, afternoon.
78. Rudolf Steiner, GA 143, lecture of 8 May 1912.
79. Ibid.
80. Rudolf Steiner, GA 116, lecture of 8 February 1910. (Author's emphasis.)
81. See in this connection Peter Selg, *Rudolf Steiner und das Fünfte Evangelium. Eine Studie*, Dornach 2005.
82. Rudolf Steiner, GA 148, lecture of 18 December 1913.
83. Rudolf Steiner, GA 152, lecture of 14 October 1913.
84. Ibid., lecture of 2 May 1913.
85. See in this connection Rudolf Steiner, *Der Baugedanke des Goetheanum. Einleitender Vortrag mit Erklärungen zu den Lichtbildern des Goetheanum-Baues*, Bern, 29 June 1921, Dornach 1986.
86. Rudolf Steiner, GA 233, lecture of 31 December 1923.
87. Rudolf Steiner, GA 121, lecture of 7 June 1910.
88. Rudolf Steiner, GA 130, lecture of 4 November 1911.
89. For more on Christ as the future 'Lord of Karma', see in particular Rudolf Steiner's Karlsruhe lectures on 7 and 14 October 1911 (GA 131) as well as the Nuremberg account on 2 December 1911 (GA 130).
90. See in this context Peter Selg, *Die Kultur der Selbstlosigkeit*, pp. 40 ff.
91. See Rudolf Steiner, *Der Baugedanke des Goetheanum. Einleitender Vortrag mit Erklärungen zu den Lichtbildern des Goetheanum-Baues*, Bern, 29 June 1921.
92. See Rudolf Steiner, GA 118.
93. Rudolf Steiner, GA 159, lecture of 18 May 1915.
94. Quoted in Friedrich Rittelmeyer, *Meine Lebensbegegnung mit Rudolf Steiner*, p. 79.
95. Rudolf Steiner, GA 229, lecture of 7 October 1923.
96. Quoted by Willem Zeylmans van Emmichoven, see Peter Selg: *Anfänge anthroposophischer Heilkunst*, Dornach 2000, p. 191.

97. As early as 14 May 1912, Rudolf Steiner said in Berlin: 'Yes, even the outward portrayal of the image of Christ, the way his outward form should be pictured, is a question that still needs to be resolved. Human souls on earth will inevitably experience many feelings when, alongside all the attempts made through the ages, is to come another that will, in some degree, show what the Christ is as supersensible impetus that enters evolution on earth. Previous attempts did not get anywhere near such a portrayal of Christ. What must emerge is an externalized expression, a manifestation formed and structured from within by impulses of wonder, compassion and conscience. What comes to expression in this way must render the countenance of Christ so alive that we see how what makes us into human beings on earth, the qualities of sensory desire and drive, is overcome by what spiritualizes the countenance. There must be the very greatest strength in the countenance through the fact that everything one can imagine as the highest development of conscience is revealed in the details of chin and mouth—a mouth of which one feels that it is not there for eating but instead for expressing the greatest morality and conscience that has ever been cultivated in humanity. This is the impression one must gain from the whole skeletal system, from the teeth and lower jaw forming the mouth. This will come to expression in such a face. Such strength will be connected with this lower part of the countenance that it radiates through, dismembers and reconfigures the whole of the rest of the human body so that it assumes a different form, and that in consequence other forces in turn are also overcome. It will therefore be impossible to give the figure of Christ who has a mouth such as I have described the kind of physical form that modern human beings have. Instead one will have to give him eyes from which speaks the highest power of compassion with which it is possible for eyes to look on other beings: not eyes that receive impressions but which instead enter utterly into others' joys and sufferings. And he

will have a forehead which refutes any sense that, within it, earthly sense impressions are thought. Instead his forehead, which will somewhat overhang the eyes, will arch over that part of the brain. Yet this will not be a 'thinker's forehead' that processes what is already there. Instead, overhanging the eyes and gently arching backwards over the head, it will express wonder, what one may call wonder at the mysteries of the world. This will have to be a head that one could not encounter amongst physical humanity.' (Rudolf Steiner, GA 133.)

98. Ibid.
99. Peter Selg, *Rudolf Steiner und das Fünfte Evangelium. Eine Studie*, Dornach 2005.
100. See Eric Hobsbawm, *The Age of Extremes. The History of the World 1914–1991*, Vintage Books, 1996.
101. Rudolf Steiner, GA 152, lecture of 14 October 1913.
102. 'He pointed to the garment. "If it were to be properly depicted, it should be of streaming love alone." ' (Willem Zeylmans van Emmichoven in: M. J. Krück von Poturzyn (ed.), *Wir erlebten Rudolf Steiner. Erinnerungen seiner Schüler*, p. 255.
103. See the relevant accounts by Rudolf Steiner in Peter Selg, *Edith Maryon, Rudolf Steiner und die Dornacher Christus-Plastik*, pp. 79 ff.
104. Rudolf Steiner, GA 260, lecture of 31 December 1923.
105. Rudolf Steiner, GA 229, lecture of 7 October 1923.
106. In relation to the reality of the world-creative capacity of the moral will, of in particular Rudolf Steiner, see GA 202.
107. Rudolf Steiner, GA 260, lecture of 25 December 1923.
108. Rudolf Steiner, GA 229, lecture of 7 October 1923.
109. See in this connection Peter Selg, *Vom Umgang mit Rudolf Steiner's Werk. Ursprung, Krise und Zukunft des Dornacher Goetheanum*. Dornach 2007, pp. 59 and 112 ff.; see also: Peter Selg, *Rudolf Steiner und die Freie Hochschule für Geisteswissenschaft. Die Begründung der 'Ersten Klasse'*, Arlesheim 2008.

110. Rudolf Steiner, GA 192, lecture of 9 June 1919.

111. Christian Morgenstern, *Werke und Briefe*, Stuttgart edition with commentary, vol. II, Stuttgart 1992, p. 204.

112. Eight-page, typed manuscript with handwritten corrections by Assya Turgeniev. Headed: 'A. Turgeniev Bugaiev Dornach 1928, From the work on the Group (?)' The estate of Assya Turgeniev, Ita Wegman Institute for Basic Research into Anthroposophy, Arlesheim, and Rudolf Steiner Archive, Dornach. I am indebted to Frau Vala Rickoff for allowing this first publication of the manuscript and for making available various materials from the estate of Assya Turgeniev. The manuscript was published here without stylistic editing. Decades later, Assya Turgeniev included passages from the manuscript in her text: *Erinnerungen an Rudolf Steiner und die Arbeit am ersten Goetheanum*, Stuttgart 1972.

Bibliography of Works by Rudolf Steiner

KEY

AP/SB = Anthroposophic Press/SteinerBooks, USA
RSP   = Rudolf Steiner Press, UK

GA 13   *Occult Science, An Outline* (RSP)
GA 15   *The Spiritual Guidance of the Individual and Humanity* (AP)
GA 40   *Wahrspruchworte*
GA 92   *Grundelemte der Esoterik*
GA 116   *The Christ Impulse and the Development of the Ego Consciousness* (RSP)
GA 118   *Das Ereignis der Christus-Erscheinung in der ätherischen Welt*
GA 121   *The Mission of the Individual Folk Souls in Relation to Teutonic Mythology* (RSP)
GA 127   *Die Mission der neuen Geistesoffenbarung. Das Christus-Ereignis als Mittelpunktsgeschehen der Erdenevolution*
GA 130   *Esoteric Christianity and the Mission of Christian Rosenkreutz* (RSP)
GA 131   *From Jesus to Christ* (RSP)
GA 133   *Earthly and Cosmic Man* (Rudolf Steiner Publishing Co.)
GA 143   *Erfahrungen des Übersinnlichen. Die drei Wege der Seele zu Christus*
GA 148   *The Fifth Gospel* (RSP)
GA 152   *Approaching the Mystery of Golgotha* (SB)
GA 155   *Christus und die menschliche Seele. Über den Sinn des Lebens*
GA 157   *The Destinies of Individuals and of Nations* (RSP)
GA 159   *Das Geheimnis des Todes. Wesen und Bedeutung Mitteleuropas und die europäischen Volksgeister*

GA 165   *Die geistige Vereinigung der Menschheit durch den Christus-Impuls*

GA 175   *Bausteine zu einer Erkenntnis des Mysteriums von Golgotha* (RSP)

GA 178   *Secret Brotherhoods* (RSP)

GA 192   *Education as a Force for Social Change* (SB)

GA 198   *Heilfaktoren für den sozialen Organismus*

GA 200   *The New Spirituality and the Christ Experience* (RSP)

GA 202   *Der Mensch in Zusammenhang mit dem Kosmos*

GA 204   *Materialism and the Task of Anthroposophy* (AP)

GA 211   *The Sun Mystery and the Mystery of Death and Resurrection* (SB)

GA 226   *Menschenwesen, Menschenschicksal und Welt-Entwickelung*

GA 229   *Das Miterleben des Jahreslaufes in vier kosmischen Imaginationen*

GA 233   *World History in the Light of Anthroposophy* (RSP)

GA 255b   *Die Anthroposophie und ihre Gegner 1919–1921*

GA 259   *Das Schicksalsjahr 1923 in der Geschichte der Anthroposophischen Gesellschaft: Vom Goetheanumbrand zur Weihnachtstagung*

GA 260   *The Christmas Conference for the Foundation of the General Anthroposophical Society 1923–1924* (RSP/AP)

GA 268   *Mantrische Sprüche. Seelenübungen II. 1903–1925*

GA 286   *Architecture as a Synthesis of the Arts* (RSP)

Ita Wegman Institute

for Basic Research into Anthroposophy

PFEFFINGER WEG 1 A CH-4144 ARLESHEIM, SWITZERLAND

www.wegmaninstitut.ch

The Ita Wegman Institute for Basic Research into Anthroposophy is a non-profit research and teaching organization. It undertakes basic research into the lifework of Dr. Rudolf Steiner (1861–1925) and the application of Anthroposophy in specific areas of life, especially medicine, education, and curative education. Work carried out by the Institute is supported by a number of foundations and organizations and an international group of friends and supporters. The Director of the Institute is Prof. Dr. Peter Selg.